Revolution of psychology

Being human

Black consciousness

Human consciousness

Universal consciousness

Religion

Liberation

Revolution of psychology

Psyche is a Greek term for soul, mind or spirit, and logy mean study of. Psychology is the study of the mind or the study of the way one thinks. It is also the study of the soul or spirit. These simple terms have always been the cause of so much confusion among us. Anything that can’t be perceived with the five senses is spirit. The mind is spirit, it part of us. Everyone knows they are thinking. Yet no one has ever seen his own thoughts. We can see images in our minds but the thinking process just happens. The soul is the sum of all spiritual attributes pertaining to the individual being.

Revolution of Psychology is a complete change in ways of thinking, of perceiving the self.

As African we have got used to a way of thinking that is so detrimental to our wellbeing. The perception of an African, a black African in particular, even by Africans themselves is that of a poor, worthless human being who is not even aware he exists. We see ourselves as inferior in most cases. As an example a south African MP once said that every time he was accompanied by a white guard all doors were wide opened wherever he went. But if he was assigned a black body guard, the poor guard would have to announce the MP’s arrival with very long explanations. Very often was denied entry in some places. Have you seen the way we receive white visitors in our houses or countries? But when an African man goes to Europe, he will be searched for hours as if he is going to steal the country.

From the beginning of colonialism, we were forced to abandon our ways of being. Languages were forced upon us, a whole culture destroyed. Our cultures were qualified as primitives, our ancestors forced to abandon their villages to go work in mines, to build roads for their western invaders.

As a consequence, today it is common to see Africans who can't even speak their own mother tongues, priding themselves as being doctors in the English language, French language, Italian, Spanish..., where have we ever seen a doctor in the Swahili language, or Zulu, Xhosa, Lingala?

Of all the slaves in suits in the world, we have never heard of single one who decided to go and build his villages of origin. We all are proud to be called doctor, engineer, minister…, going back to the village to show off our big degrees; and that we see every day.

We are known to be very intelligent, very physically strong. We have built countries in the world under the watchful eye of our slave masters. But why haven't we built anything significant for ourselves in Africa? Most constructions where left by our colonisers. After they left we still follow them to Europe so they can still tell us what to do.

The African exodus, today, is leaving the doors open to thieves of all kind, carrying peace keeping and united nation flags. They have managed to corrupt many of our African brothers who, unfortunately are willingly selling their own for a less than penny.

No black African wants to be associated with Africa. It is an African dream to go and live in Europe or America, to sound like them, to look like them. No matter how expensive we dress, how expensive we drink, no matter how expensive we live, we will never be white. We can imitate but it will be to no avail.

For our ladies, extensions, wigs, make up will not make you white. It is just trying to be something we are not. No matter how hard we try, no matter much money we have, with or without a suit, in their eyes, we will for ever be the same primitive savages they once found in the bush.

Is it not time we started thinking of reviving our cultures? I mean our true cultures, the culture that if we do not fight to conserve like the Tibetans in exile, will end up disappearing, like the red Indians in America, like the Aborigines in Australia. We will be found working like slaves in our own countries, working jobs that should not even be in existence. Go to Cape town waterfront where you will find black people from all over Africa, slaving themselves to serve Europeans.

Killing out of jealousy, pride, greed; Loosing virginity at 9 years of age, rape, Child molestation, Selfishness, theft.

All these are found in our poor communities and they are just a consequence of the loss of a sense of self. A clear sign of mind degeneration. A mind devoid of divine connection and self-purpose. A mind trying to adopt and nurture ways of living that may seem appealing, be it good or bad, to puts food on the table and survives to see another day. Once the culture, the religion, the morality is removed the mind has the adapt to something new to survive. Unfortunately, the only culture, religion, morality we can learn from the white man is **money**.

By culture, I mean replacing the lack of culture, of traditional religion, of morality with ancient African wisdom. The African grand masters of ancient time still hold the key to their knowledge, reserved only for those with clarity of purpose. **Ubuntu** is also known as dharma in the east.

But it is not hopeless. It just means that it time to start reversing the wrong way of thinking that got us here.

Instead of waiting for another person to come and build on our land while we are in exile, due to a bad economic situation, we should think of starting to rebuild our culture, and relive them. Teach them to the young ones for generations to come. That culture is Ubuntu. There is a secret meaning embedded in this word. This word doesn't just define how one should live in the community but also his connection with all that is, was and will ever be.

It is really sad to see young people, lured by the promise of a few monetary notes, dance and sing their lungs out to please their western visitors, tourists, under the pretence of showing their culture. Culture is something that is lived every day, the way one walk, speaks, eats, the respect shown to all fellow man. Not some dance aimed at pleasing a person so they can throw a few coins in your beggar's hat. Have you ever heard of an American or European dancing for an African just because they went to visit them? On the contrary they try their best to make you feel like you don't belong.

“what is the purpose of your visit?” Remember that sentence at all at the airports and border gates? in Europe and America of course.

In Africa we say:” welcome, make yourself at home.” to everyone, even thieves.

This book is in no way racist. It is just a call to our brothers to awake and be conscious of themselves and claim what is rightfully theirs: their consciousness. Our land can be stolen; our mineral can be stolen but our divine consciousness can’t. we just need to remember to be.

It a call for the African to remember who they are, to remember where they really come from, to be members of society who bring a positive contribution to the world at large, to unlock what has been hidden within due to a wrong way of thinking about themselves.

Being human

Happiness!!! Every human being on planet earth wants to be happy. But we all seem to be in pursuit of that word constantly. A lot of us find temporary relief from pain, problems and after a short while the chase continuous. We seem to confuse relief for happiness. In the end the majority of us die exhausted, wondering what consumed us so much that we never noticed the simple things in life that actually make us happy, content. For example, a young man's dream is to finish his studies. As soon as he gets his degree his will be very happy for a day. Then comes to stress of getting a job and getting experience. Once he gets a job he will be happy for a day. Then there will the house, the car, the wife, the kids. It never ends. He thinks he will be happy by acquiring one thing only to find out that happiness will be short live because the next thing to make him happy is awaiting. In ancient Africa being happy meant having a healthy relationship with fellow human beings and nature. Being aware of the fact that there is higher being who is above us, worshiping him by showing respect to the whole of his creation.

The four basic activities common to all living entities on this planet are: eating, sleeping, reproducing and defending. Once these four basic needs are met then as human beings we can say that we are happy. From there we can evolve within until we become permanently happy and joyful.

It is very difficult to explain what life is exactly. We can only live it, experience it. Where there is life we experience motion, which brings about change. Changing into something better or bigger is called growth. It is an innate need of every human to grow. We always want the next best thing. We want a bigger house, a bigger car...

As human beings we want to grow. Growth that brings about permanent happiness, begins within and manifest without. This simple basic truth when applied to the life of any individual bring about miracles and it is a fundamental truth that the entire planet earth knows and that the African was denied. The whole world knows that it is the peace within that brings about wealth. Once inner peace is reached outer peace follows. In Africa we are told to chase after wealth first, then we will find peace. Many of us opted for studies of a profession that pays well rather than a profession that would make us feel at peace. Many rich African people are miserable. The can't sleep at night because of the ill manner in which they had acquired their wealth.

The meaning of the cross symbol seen everywhere is not exclusively Christian, it is universal and one of the many interpretations of this sacred symbol is growth on the horizontal path which is external and visible, and the vertical path which internal and hidden.

Western education applies only to external aspect of the individual with the exception of philosophy, psychology. In simple terms, education we get from school only gives pointers on how to live comfortable lives and how to behave in society. Once a person has completed their studies the are guaranteed a comfortable and good paying jobs, that's all. Growth in this instance means promotion or changing carriers in order to earn more or have a more comfortable job. As consequence with better pay we get a better house, a better car, going on vacation, earning more respect for the good things we possess.

The only way people try to connect with the inner self and grow within is through religion. The unfortunate truth is even religion itself as we know it, on the African continent, has been concocted in order to facilitate colonization. For example, there is speech of king Leopold2 of Belgium addressing the missionaries, priests and pastors in the Congo in the 1980's. Here is the direct translation from a French video:

" Reverent fathers, pastors and dear compatriots. Welcome to our great Belgium-Congo country. The

task that been assigned to you is very delicate and requires great tactical skills. Priests and pastors, you have come to preach indeed, but that preaching is inspired from our great principle: first and foremost, the interest of our metropolis. The real purpose of your mission is not to teach the black men how to know God, they know him already from their ancestors. They pray and worship Nzambe Mpunu and Nzambe Mawezi… They know that killing, stealing, sleeping with a another man's wife, swear …is bad. Let have the courage to admit that what we have not come to teach them what they know already. This means you will interpret the gospels in ways that serve your interests in this part of the world. You will make sure that those blacks savages do not take any interests in the wealth that is underground on their land. so that they would never awake and create a deadly competition. Your experience in the gospel should help you find verses that recommends, makes one love poverty. For example," happy be the poor for the kingdom of heaven belongs to them.", "it is as difficult for rich man to enter the kingdom of heaven as it is for a camel to go through a needle eye" you will do everything in your power to make sure the nigger get scared of getting rich so they can go to heaven. You will give them very little support so they would never start a rebellion one day. The industrious and the administrator will conform themselves to what I'm recommending to you, white priests and pastors.

From time to time, you will insult, beat to make yourselves feared so they would never resort to violence. It must never happen that the nigger retaliates and tries to take revenge. For that you will teach them by all means, you will insist on following the examples of all the saints who gave their chicks to be slapped, who forgave the trespasses, who got spat on, who got beaten up. You must discourage and detach them from what could give them the courage to confront us. Here referring especially to their war witchcraft, that they pretend not to want to leave behind.

Your actions will focus mostly on the young ones so they would never hesitate to great us. If the actions of the priest is against the word, insist that they should be submissive and obedient blindly. You must teach the students to believe not to think. Here are some of the principles you will apply without fail. You will find a lot more in the books you will receive at the end of this session. You will see what I recommend to you white priests and pastors. Preach them to the bone so they would never revolt against the injustices they will suffer by your hand. Make them recite everyday: "happy are those who are suffering, for the kingdom of heaven is theirs "whip them, keep their wives at the mission for 9 months, and sleep with them if you want to, make them work for you. Make them convert into Christians and as a token of gratitude, they must bring their good meat, chickens, eggs. Do everything you can to make sure the black man never gets rich. To achieve this, you must tell them every day that it is impossible for a rich man to go to heaven. Make them pay a tax every Sunday in church and use that money (supposed to go to the poor) to create beautiful stores where you are. Build nice parishes, transform your places of missions and create big flourishing shopping centres and then help lightly the poor. All this to encourage other white men to come and invest. Ask the black man to die of hunger while you eat 5 times a day. Your stomach should always be full of good foods until you mouth burps the smell of onions. Create a system a detection of any black man who would ever think of demanding their national independence. Teach a doctrine that you will not practice and if they asked you why you are not practicing what you are preaching, tell them that "you blacks do as you are told not as I do" and if they say "faith with no actions is dead faith." get angry and beat them. And reply "happy are those who believe without questioning".

Tell them that the statues you are keeping in your houses are the works of Satan, use those statues to fill up your museums. Make the black man forget his ancestors, so they can worship yours who will always look after them. For example, saint Mary, saint Therese, Saint Martin. Make them pray by making them kneel before you, make them recite the Rosary ten times or more a day. Never give a chair to a black man who comes to visit you. Never invite them at least give them a cigarette. Never invite them to eat with you even if they slaughter a rooster or a chicken every time you visit them.

By doing this our country Belgium will be rich. It is only later that they will come to understand that we were not helping them for the love of God."

The king of Belgium LEOPOLD 2.

As you can see, growth within does not come from sitting in church every Sunday. what we can achieve by sitting in church is just making one charlatan rich, one who calls himself a pastor. We were more connected to the divine through our African indigenous beliefs than we will ever be by going to church. I will try my best to demonstrate that there is actually no better way of believing in divine. All forms of schools of thought are indeed the same in essence. It is also true that there is handful of man who abuse religion but turning it into a money making scam.

Authentic religion and the moral code is society defines how a we think. The black African man way of thinking has been engineered through a concocted religious believes. It is very wrong. Being human entails being able to think freely. A human being is an intellectual animal. thinking, imagining is his birth right. No one should have to enforce his way of thinking or beliefs upon another. Removing that basic right, is to remove humanity out of him which makes him an animal. An animal who would chase after any shining thing you would throw in front of it. Is it not what the black African is doing?

The modern African man is a slave of money. Slavery and colonization hasn't ended yet. We are just living the aftermath of those systems. In fact, it might even be worse now that no chains or whips are no longer being used. The new system is to make us voluntarily accept slavery as normal through the use of money. We chase after money. The white man uses money to make his dreams come true. These 2 scenarios are very different. In the first instance a few notes are being thrown in front of us and we blindly follow, it doesn't matter where we going, don't care, call it salary. In the second he owns money. How many rich black people became broke in a matter of days? As long as the owner of money is satisfied you are safe but if he is not you lose everything. If you don't believe me, read the papers. The correct way to perceive money is that it is the result of work performed correctly. It is just an energy that is used to express oneself through his work. It is a result not an end.

A human being who know himself should not run after money by killing and stealing but money should rather run after him as a result of the good work that he is able to produce. The unnatural way of thinking that characterizes the back African, was engineered and must be broken.

It is his right to think that the science of thinking created by our ancestor spread out throughout the world, one of its products is Christianity which in essence is a science of thinking right. It is time to be human again, it is time to start thinking right.

When it comes to evolving within one should teach himself to rely on his instinct. The beginning of thinking right is meditation. Trying to calm the mind in order to perceive the inner voice. All forms of religions only point at the inner self. The purpose of all life is help the dormant inner being to awake and evolve, to be what it was before the creation of this material world.

Being human means being able to evolve on the vertical and horizontal lines at the same time. That is proper growth.

Black consciousness

Brothers and sisters, being black is not a curse, it doesn't mean one has to be poor, doesn't mean that one has to live at the bottom of the money ladder. It doesn't mean you have to wake up every morning to go and beg for alms.

It only means your skin colour is black. It is beautiful as it is. No more, no less.

Every single one of us walking on the road is a consciousness locked in a human body. When you wake up in the morning, don't you ever have the impression that you are sitting inside your human machine and driving it? Most of the time when you are busy, the colour of your skin does not really matter. It is only what you are doing that matters in that moment. All you want is to be happy like everyone else.

We waste so much time trying to avoid being associated with the stigma given to the word black: Darkness, evil, thief, poor, starving, ugly, even Satan has been painted black. We thing happiness is achievable only by avoiding being black, it is heart breaking truly. You don't believe me?

I will give a few instances: as soon as a black man gets rich he doesn't want to be associated with black. They go as far as buying a house in a white area, where they would pay 10 times as much as a white person. They won't hesitate marring a white woman so the children won't have to suffer blackness.

Why do you think women consider themselves beautiful only when they wear long artificial hair and bleach their skin? As if being dark with short bushy hair is an abomination.

Let try and unlock the black mystery. If you did not know the first richest people to inhabit planet earth were black, the pharaohs of Egypt were black. We are their descendants, all Bantu ethnic groups moved from the north after the desertification of the Sahara region. All we know of them today is that their tombs were raided. The thieves are probably the richest families on earth. That because our ancestors were buried with unimaginable wealth. Some tombs were estimated to be worth 200.0000.000 us dollars. And one of the most ancient sacred books are exposed in museums, the Egyptian book of the dead, but they will never be deciphered unless one the children of this soil decides to unlock the mysteries for the benefit of this world.

The black man has never been poor throughout history. No, no, no.

He has been wealthy and wise unfortunately for them they were too friendly to anyone who wanted to visit this land. They opened the door to thieves. Ubuntu teaches us to be kind to all living beings. we to thought that the white man is our friend. Once they settled hey turned out to be evil. Most the priests were the first ones to be killed and kings corrupted. The westerner made himself God and enslaved the rest of Africa. Where force could not be used, false religion was introduced. We were forced to believe our role model is from the west. We were forced to believe we were beneath him but the time has come to review what we have been taught as being true. But this time let not try to have an intellectual debate. Let use what we were taught from time immemorial to unlock the mysteries of the self, of who the black man is.

The gold that the west is fighting for today, that they found in Africa, south America, Asia, India, Spain was not dug out. If you have ever heard of the word alchemy, the mother of chemistry, the science that sought to change any matter into gold. We had many who could change any matter into what they wanted it to be. The ancient African man knew the science of changing matter into gold. He had true magic at his fingertips. Magic that we were told was witchcraft. The real gold is not matter. It lays in our true values, transmitted from father to son, mother to daughter. Values that the west has never been able to steal. The true golden man lays within each of us. The relationship that we had with nature conferred to power to bring matter to life at will.

Most of us today turn into buffoons when we surrounded by whites, we speak the loudest, show off our dancing skills, try to show off all the few talents we possess or even that we can dress better just to get a little appreciation. How can you dress better than the one who makes your clothes, or be richer than the one who owns the bank you save your money in?

Being real black man is to be true to the self within. We connected to the self through dance and music. We connected to the self through our ancestors. They are not evil, they are not witchcraft, they are the same being that are called angels, faeries, jinn's, demigods. Why should the same word mean evil just because it is called in an African language?

Trinity: God the father, the son, holy spirit. Brahman, Shiva, Vishnu. Watch the shock when I say Osiris, Isis, Horus. Just because it is of African origin doesn't mean it is evil. It just means there are three divine forces that help man regain his true identity among the beings in superior worlds, Among the ancestors.

Whether the skin is white, black, yellow, red the human body is just a prison. No matter how much one is enjoying his life, the body is just holding a soul. The soul yearns to return to it source. Judging one on the basis of the skin colour is absurd.

Through the many lives we have lived we have changed countless skin colours, shapes and forms. It like sitting in a vehicle. The five senses only help us connect to the world and we connect to the universe through 7 inner senses or chakras. when the vehicle grows old we change it.

The only reason the black man is led to believe he is inferior is because of the wealth underground, not because of the way he looks or the way he lives. He is hated because of the wealth he has always possessed throughout history. Why did they have to cut off the sphinx's nose just so we may think the statue had a pointy nose? Isn't it taking it a bit too far. All the wealth in the northern part of Africa, including material and spiritual books belonged to the black Africans of ancient times. Here I'm referring to Timbuktu in Mali. Here is an article from the *African echo* newspaper, may 30th 2019

University of Timbuktu-The first University in the world

Did you know the first university

in the World was located in AFRICA? Please read on.

Sankore University Campus

The University was organized around three great Masajids or Mosques. The Masajid of Jingaray Ber, The Masajid of Sidi Yahya, The Masajid of Sankore. Masajids are places of worship for Muslims. Not only did students seek knowledge, but they also purified their souls through the sciences of Islam. Islam breeds leaders that are God fearing, just, honest, trustworthy and of excellent moral character. Graduate students were the embodiment of the teachings of the Holy Qur'an and the traditions of the Mohammed, the Prophet of Islam.

Around the 12th century, the University of Timbuktu had an attendance of 25, 000 students in a city which had a population of 100, 000 people. The students came from all corners of the African continent in search of excellence in knowledge and trade. On graduation day, students were given Turbans. The turban symbolizes Divine light, wisdom, knowledge and excellent moral conduct. The turban represents the demarcation line between knowledge and ignorance. The knots and circles of the turban represent the name Allah. This means that the graduate students know the Divine obligations and responsibilities to be discharge honorably in their communities and toward their fellowmen.

Manuscripts from the University

A lecturere with students

The university was organised in 4 levels. The primary level which was basically based on the Holy Qur'an. The secondary level imparted virtues of life, The third level was research under the feet of reknowned professors and the fourth level known as the circle of knowledge introduced students to the wisdom Muslim Imams, Scholars and Professors parted with.

The rulers and caliphs or Muslims state leaders such as Askia Mohammed of the Songhai Empire, Mansa Musa of the Malian Empire, Shayk Amadu of the Fulani caliphate of Massina, The Amirs and sultans of the provinces of the Sudan often sent crucial questions to the Ulemas or scholars of Timbuktu for solutions.

Africa has a rich past that needs to be echoed. The question of what happened ought to be answered and answered quickly...

Here is another article from the south African history online 12-july-2016

successful empires in the world?

The Mali Empire controlled all of the salt trade along the trade routes and was the second largest and most successful empire between 1230 and 1600.

The Niger River

The Niger River played an important part in Mali's success, providing a method of transporting heavy goods and accessing more trade. The river also made the soil more fertile, which led to better crops and better feed to raise livestock.

Some of the most commonly grown crops included beans, cotton, gourds, millet, papaya, peanuts, rice and sorghum. Livestock included cattle, goats, poultry and sheep.

Economy

All goods had to be heavily taxed and all gold nuggets were declared property of the king, leaving only gold dust to be traded. The Empire also offered protection against conflict that started along the trade routes. As the Empire expanded, salt, cotton cloth, gold and later cowrie shells were used as currency.

Mansa Musa

Known as the King of Kings, Mansa Musa was one of the most successful and wealthy leaders of the Kingdom of Mali. He ruled in the early 1300's until his death in 1337. Many of the palaces and Mosques built during his reign can still be seen today. He had an estimated worth of 400 billion US dollars and even though he lived so long ago, he is still said to be the wealthiest man of all time.

Being called primitive has its advantages such as being connected to the universe. How much money do people spend today just to try and live like the so called savages? Isn't organic food primitive?

The disrespect we show to planet earth today causes so much

imbalances that we are seeing: global warming. Mother earth is alive. The metals within her womb are her veins and arteries. They are also the senses she uses to connect and communicate with other planets. If you thought gravity and magnetism alone are the cause of her being suspended in space, think again. Maybe someday science will prove that mother earth navigates intelligently through the milky way. We dig without restriction as long as the Man is making money. Each planet has a dominant metal within and that its signature. The different vibrations frequencies sent and received from other planets also greatly influence us, our moods, even the weather. The metals also control the heat circulation inside the earth. That is why before cutting downs a tree we used to ask the ancestors. Before digging a well, the ancestors had to be consulted. Before killing an animal, we had to ask and be grateful after the hunt. Call it primitive, I call intelligent.

The same clever chicken that we used to chase for hours so it can be slaughtered in the villages, is the same one you will buy from the supermarket for 10 times the price. Why not grow your own flock in the village make the money for yourself, peacefully, instead of slaving yourself in big towns? That is because we don’t believe in us. That is because most of us are being taught we can only live under the wing of the white supremacy.

This kind of thinking should change.

Human consciousness

A myth is a story invented to explain natural phenomenon's. Some of our African stories have been turned into myths just to confuse us. Myth or no myth, it is the profound meaning of the story that really matters. Here is a true magical story, from a kid's stories website:

The story of Isis and Osiris

Egypt, Egypt

Osiris was believed to be an Egyptian Pharaoh who reigned over Egypt in the very early beginnings. Osiris married his sister Isis and they ruled

Egypt together. Osiris helped people learn how to grow crops along the river Nile. Osiris and Isis became very popular with subjects.

Seth Osiris's and Isis's brother was cruel and jealous of Osiris. Seth married her sister Nephthys. But with the light came darkness. Seth was trying to kill Osiris with a plan. Seth had with him his wicked companions. They came with a plan to kill Osiris, they prepared his coffin for Osiris. Isis was full of wisdom and magic and kept a close eye over her love.

Seth held a banquet honor of the Divine Pharaoh Osiris and invited 72 conspirators, with the finest banquet to be held in Egypt. When Osiris heart was warm of joy, Seth brought the coffin and told him to try it. Osiris went inside the coffin to try it, Seth closed the lid of the coffin and nailed it with no people around. He went to the Nile with his wicked conspirators and the coffin, they threw the coffin in the Nile. The coffin bashed on a tree on land, and the tree became beautiful as the body of Osiris touched the tree. The tree grew so big that it hid the coffin.

The king Malcander and Queen Astarte of Byblos saw this tree and ordered it to be cut down and made into a beautiful pillar. When Isis heard about her husband's death she was distraught and set off to find her husband body as Seth took the throne. She traveled a lot until she reached the city Byblos. Isis meet some maidens and taught them to braid their hair. They were serving the Queen Astarte and the queen saw the girl's hair and she was so impressed that she called for Isis. Unaware that the woman Astarte had called forth was the Divine Goddess Isis she asked for caring for her son, Dictys. Isis consented and after a short while she caught sight of the pillar.

In time Isis realized that the great pillar held the body of her beloved husband. She had also become fond of the young Dictys and so one night decided to make him immortal. With her spell she transformed into a swallow and chanted her magic words the Queen Astarte has been spying on her and in horror interrupted the spell in fear at the sight of her baby son in flames. The spell was broken. When the Queen realized she begged the Goddess for forgiveness and asked there was anything she could do. Isis asked for the pillar and so were re -joined with her husband's body. When Osiris's body had returned home Isis was forced to hide it.

Unfortunately an irate Seth discovered the body and in his rage cut it into 14 pieces and scattered it down the Nile once more. Once more Isis set of in search of the body parts along with her sister Nephtys and her nephew Anubis. Whenever they found a piece of the body the place became a holy shrine. They found all but one piece. Once Isis had gathered all the pieces she magically re-built Osiris's body and even though he was dead, she was also able to magically conceive a child with him: the young Sky God Horus.

As Horus grew Osiris visited him from the spirit world and taught him how to fight in preparation in defeating Seth and retaking his right throne. After much battling with Seth Horus prevailed and avenged his mother and father.
Horus became new Pharaoh of Egypt. Isis and Osiris were in time reunited. Osiris became the God of the underworld and Isis Goddess of magic and motherhood.

There are many variations this story. But the important thing is to learn to perceive the truth within the story or the myth. The similarities between the story of Mary, mother of Jesus and the one above are mind blowing.

As an African I would rather use this myth to attempt to understand what is self-realization and ultimately God realization. Many westerners have attempted to tell this story but few actually know what it means.

Man is not complete. In the beginning, at the moment of creation he was. He was I. just as the bible say it “I am that I am”. I the same symbol use for number one in Greek and roman numerology. But after receiving a human form man becomes divided into three parts. For creation to take place there has to be motion. The law is for motion to takes place there has to be a positive source and a negative destination. The original whole remains complete but two points must be created, one full and the other empty. The side that is full always seeks to pour its bounty in the empty side to regain the balance in the whole. Take two buckets, one full of water and the other empty. Connect them with a short hose pipe at the bottom, the full one will empty its water into the second, until they have the same amount of water. Take two rooms next to each other separated by door. Heat up the one and cool down the other, open the door and the hot one will pour out the heat into the cold until the cold reaches the same temperature.

Me, myself and I. "I" is the real person, me the human body and myself the ego. In the word self, as in selfish, is the cause of what drives us away from the I, from whatever is divine within us. The I being divine in nature is the same in the microcosm (man) and the macrocosm(God).

The myself is subdivided into many personalities. We all have many selves that we need to attend to within us. Pride, envy, anger, greed, gluttony, wrath and sloth. They are the personification of the 7 main egos or my-selves. They are vices that possess opposite virtues which are in turn also false selves, In total 14. the real self has nothing to do with pride or humility, envy and compassion, … the real self within only follows the orders of the father.

Trinity, the concept that is in all religions that divides God the father in 3: father, mother and son. Father, son and holy spirit. Osiris, Isis,

Horus. Brahman, Shiva, Vishnu. The trinity has its replica within the human being. As above so below.

I am angry, I am jealous, I'm lazy... The real self the" I am" is just is. The attributes afterwards are the descriptions of the different egos. Here it is necessary to introduce a different number four. three represents stability or the multiple perfect unity. Without the fourth forces there is no need for the trinity to exist. four is the real negative force. two and three are created to bring back the balance of the whole. four is there to test the stability of the whole. Having this in mind let return to the story.

The mother (Isis within) loves her husband (Osiris within), the real self. she seeks to eliminate the illusion of the false I's (Seth has created) until the real "I am" remains. She seeks within the dessert of our inner chaos to find the different parts of the self until the day we will be complete. You can call her mother nature, divine mother, Mary, Yashoda, Isis it doesn't matter.

The human body is given to us as a gift, no matter what the colour. The main purpose is for the soul inside to live through experiences that will make grow. Our soul is a direct manifestation of the divine.

God is one energy with many names. The relationship we have with our creator varies depending on our level of awareness. God can be perceived as a father, mother or even son.

The human and the animal bodies functions are very similar. Their functions are eating, sleeping, reproducing and defending. Life is a fight to meet those four basic needs. Above that, man seeks to find his higher purpose. Man will seek to find his purpose in his job, his relationships and other things if he is not guided properly.

The African man mistakenly adopted the western culture as his way of life and higher purpose. Every man on this continent wants to achieve their dreams like their western counterparts. When you try to find out what their dreams or purposes in life are, the answer is surely to have a lot of money, to be able to afford a better life.

Man was born in sin, in other words in ignorance. He wonders through life trying to find his purpose through his job, his relationships, his activities. Yet there is only one place where he can find all the answers: his heart. Ubuntu is the process through which a man goes to find his humanity. That includes his relationships with fellow man, living beings and the universe at large.

The connection we have with all being starts on the physical with what we perceive with the five senses. We collect information first than we reflect on what we know. Questions follow after reflexion. We can have a good job, a good life but once we see a person die, we will eventually wonder why are we living? Our earthly knowledge is enable to answer such questions.

Trying to find out what we are as human beings is the main purpose of life. When guided properly a man can't answer that question, he can only experience it.

At this point a person realises that the five senses are enough to perceive deeper truths. One need to develop a quiet mind in order to be able to use his hidden faculties. The western culture is made to keep the mind always busy. The all week people have workloads that are impossible to finish. On week-ends people want relax by keeping the mind even more occupied with movies, alcohol, clubs, drugs, sex…

Church was also created to keep one's mind busy. Connection to our creator and going to church are two different things. In Africa we find the largest church congregations, yet we are the poorest continent.

We have never manufactured a match stick on our own. Please bothers, know that connection to God is not only for Christians, but for everyone. The only thing you achieve by going to church is distraction and making one charlatan rich. Even the way we were taught to pray is wrong. We were made so dependent on the white, we always beg him for things. Even in church, we see the same thing. We just go there to beg God for things. Most of us have no idea what the words we read in the holy scriptures mean.

We need to take time off for quiet reflexion and meditation

everyday if we want to grow in our lives. There are seven energy centres along our spinal cord that we unconsciously use to connect with all beings and the universe. Those centres naturally activate once the mind is calm. That's why people go to monasteries to train their minds to calm down. A mind that is calm becomes clear. A clear mind perceives things as they are. A clear mind helps one connect with himself on a deeper level. One can see his true worth as an important part of the universe.

Ubuntu, African ancient wisdom teaches us that it takes two fingers to squish a louse. Meaning if you want to see God, look into your neighbour's eyes. We are all one. If Africa is to move forward, we have to start giving each other the value that we deserve. Slavery and colonization only succeeded because it was implanted in our heads to hate each other. Loving oneself and loving every living entity that surrounds us is Ubuntu.

That is how the complete human being is born. The true golden man, the SUN of God.

Universal consciousness

The purpose of all human beings is God realization. It is all good to tell beautiful and emotional stories. But what does it really mean in real life.
It is said:" it more difficult to conquer oneself than it is to conquer an entire country." It all begins with self-observation and merciless self-criticism, observing oneself every second of the day. That is why we meet so many people every day. Our relationships with others help us discover what we are inside.
The people we meet every day make us angry, sad, happy... It is how we react that should concern us the most. The people who bring

us the challenges are just people whether related to us or not.

It is by developing this sense of self observation that we can notice that we have anger issues or we are proud and so forth. Those defect that we notice inside of us are our inner demons that we need to fight. No one in the world should come and say they will lay their hand on you in order to remove a demon. That is a big lie. We have been victims of charlatans in Africa for too long. we are victims of crooked politicians and of false religious people.

As long as a demon of adultery is still in you, you will always fall victim to that vice and if you are a religious person you are a danger to the members of your congregation.

After discovering an inner demon also called ego, then comes the real work: Eliminating the ego. Discovering an ego alone may take a life time. Opportunities to discover an ego are not in short supply. Most of the time the same event will repeat itself in our lives in order for us to try and discover the inner cause of the of the problem. For example, a woman may fall victim to wrong man, who will just play and leave her. If she took her time and notice her inner being trying to show her the demon of greed within her, instead of looking for love she was looking wealth. It doesn't mean she has to go to some guy to pray for a nice man for her. She just needs to kill the greed in her.

Fasting has been abused among us. Every time a person is broke they fast. Whenever they go through a rough patch they fast. Real fast only is only for the purpose of killing our discovered defects.

Fast involves praying to fight our inner demons. By the power of our divine mother Isis who burned the body of Dictys to make him immortal. By burning the physical body, she was also burning all the egos. The use of the powerful prayer hail Mary is also for that purpose. *"pray for us sinners now till the hour of our death"* the death of the false self. Or in the prayer *"Christ sun of God have mercy me a sinner"*

Fasting means sacrificing all the good things that strengthen the ego like eating too much, drinking alcohol, drugs, …

Intense fast insures that a demon dies, and during that time temptation will increase too. If you were fasting to eliminate anger, you will get more and more people to make you angry. It doesn't mean you are failing; it is just that the false self doesn't want to die without a fight.

Here it is imperative to mention a misunderstood concept. The law of cause and effect. The real cause underlying every situation we are going through in life is mind. You only experience the abundance of your heart. A dirty heart causes you to live in filth. A clean heart causes you to live lavishly.

By clean or dirty I mean our most profound desires.

What we think depends on who is driving us at that time. Is it me, my-selves or I.

For example, when you wake up in the morning, you smell biscuits next door. Your gluttony wakes up; it will drive you mind to the car then to the shop so you can buy biscuits. While you are there, envy notices a nice pair of shoes on another person, it will drive you back home so you can try and wear the same pair if you have it. Let's say fear takes over and drives you to rush into the bath and go to work. These were the myselves. The me, the body may also feel cold, it will drive you wear a jacket. The I only concerns with divine matters. Praying, contemplating a beautiful scenery, …

It is by eliminating our inner demons that the true self emerges from the deep, dark pit that we call the human body, the me. As the real being is rising it awakes the latent faculties that so far have been under developed. These under developed energy centres are called Chakras.

The chakras are energy centres or senses of the inner self. The physical body has 5 senses. The inner body or the soul has 7 main ones that we never use.

The energy they create is diverted and misused. The energy becomes useful as the centres are put the good use which is receiving information and communicating with higher dimensions. We live in three dimensions and perceive the fourth in dreams. There are higher dimensions too.

We can only perceive the true magnificence of God once we our inner senses have been awakened.

"man know thyself and you will know the universe and its gods"

You can only know who you are when you there is no more ego left and you can only know the universe when all the senses to perceive it have awakened. And finally you can know God when Christ take birth within. It requires a lot of work.

Religion

Religion comes from the Latin word *Religare* meaning to bind which in turn comes from the word *Ligare* meaning to unite in harmony. Hence religion also means to re-unite in harmony. To re-unite the individual self to the universal self, man to God. They are already united they just need to be in harmony. God already live in us, black, white, red, yellow and whatever colour. The only job that has been bestowed upon man is just to awaken consciousness of God. Egos only fight us to forget who we truly are. Ultimately God is everything. The air we breathe, the water we drink, the trees, the people we see, ...everything. The law is "love others the way love yourself and love God with all your might”. whichever form of worship you choose doesn’t really matter, the true witness is the heart no one can deceive himself.

Forcing a religion on anyone is wrong.

A religion is a school of thought. A child is taught to count. He will only find out later in life that counting helps him count his salary and use his money wisely. Singing the ABC will help him read later in life. In order for a man to understand God, he has to god through practices that he doesn’t understand, religious practices. It only after he has perfected the practice and call himself a master that he rips the benefits. Practicing religious rites has its place as a training ground. Whatever method is used is not important.

The African primitive religions dating from time immemorial, which were confused with witchcraft and which we were forced to abandon were very profound. The only memory of those traditions are statues laying in museums all over the world. strange enough, those who claim there are just a form of art, are still studying them and making new discoveries about them until this day. That religious culture was swept from under our feet and rendering us faithless, helpless, and vulnerable to any form of religion, which ironical is the same as our original one devoid of it profound essence, an empty book full of confusing words. The symbol of the cross was in existence way before Christianity appeared. In the northern African tribes it looked the same with a slight difference above the horizontal line, there was a standing oval ring instead of a line.

All the religious ceremonies were practiced as well. Today many in Africa just go to church say words, sing names that were abandoned in their own villages.

I remember in my native language there is a name: Mukalai. Which is Michael.

The children of Israel that every so called Christian claim to be, actually means children **Is**is the almighty Goddess of magic and motherhood, **Ra** the sun God Amon RA, **EL** means *of God*: it is a title that you can notice in the names of people who possessed the knowledge of God. All the symbols in Christianity, the cross, the lamb, the dove, the grasshoppers with john, are painted on the walls of the pyramids dating long before the birth of Jesus. It is surprising to see that our primitive religions, all descending from the north(Egypt) got qualified as witchcraft.

We all say Amen in church not knowing that we are actually calling on the power of the sun-God Amon-RA. Oh yes, that is where the name Amen originates from, Sun of God. Son of God is an invention. We are all sons of God

As human beings we know instinctively that we need to connect to some form of higher power. The loss of our religious cultures through slavery and colonialism made vulnerable to accepting any form of worship as true. That is how we also lost our morals, and we are still trying to understand the western culture to this day. No one can truly tell what the western culture is. Democracy is not a culture, it is a method used to control the masses. It easy to start any form of movement, get everyone to believe in it and voila!!! you get votes. Even if the movement in question is detrimental to the well-being of the population.

Man, practice knowing yourself through the practice of daily meditation, allow yourself to grow within. One the most practical methods was already discussed. It taking time daily to observe oneself, eliminate egos or psychological defect within and let the inner self emerge naturally. As the self is growing it confers innate latent faculties. Of those faculties is the power to see past events, and so being able to verify what everything that was mentioned above for yourself. We have gotten so used to relying on scientific surveys to prove everything that we want to believe in. We already know everything we need to but we don't trust ourselves that's all.

Man, know yourself and you will get to know God and the universe. Reconnecting to our original self who is divine in essence is the true purpose of every human being. Our true self is part and parcel of God.

Liberation

It is the birth-right of everyone know to God no matter which religion they belong to. Africans have their religions that are very effective, that no one should under estimate and call witchcraft. Where the light shines the brightest, darkness is also densest. For every religion there is an antithesis. All religions have a negative force that will always try to eradicate it. I'm not denying that witchcraft exists. It truly powerful and it is the anti-theses of our true way of life. Because we got so lost, unfortunately those who are trying to get in touch with our true culture find themselves on the wrong side of the fence. Not knowing who is genuine in their religious cultures, especially the religious authorities.

In the struggle for survival we face every day, thinking right is the beginning of our liberation. In the maze of beliefs and cultures we need to find a way to grow inside and out. Thinking right, thinking growth and trying to reconnect are our primary concerns.

A human being has the ability to think. That usually happens when a problem arises. For example, in the past there were no houses and so people were sleeping the rain at the mercy of predators at night. They had to find a solution to that problem. They found natural caves or dug artificial ones or created huts.

The natural motion of thought is growth. Thinking about a problem mean analyzing all the possible solutions and come up with the one solution that makes us grow. As human beings it is our primary responsibility to think growth. When we are engaged in thinking about a problem, we somehow get inspired as to what the solution is and then we act on it. Thinking growth is the cause of progressive action.

This process is called creativity. When we think of what we can do in order for us to grow, we actually put ourselves in a position where we have to create a solution.

Sometimes we may not know what the solution is but certainly it will seem to come on its own. Thought has the ability to wrap itself in matter and take concrete form.

If we stop growing than we automatically start decaying.

It is imperative for us to think growth, find ways that will help us think positively. When we are thinking growth, we are thinking in accordance with the absolute truth. The reason is we are partaking in the overall creation of the universe. The truth is: creation is an ongoing process. For example, Henri Ford though of creating something to make him move faster from A to B.

every single motor vehicle we see today is one thought that keeps on growing. Every motor engineer is contributing to the growth of that same thought.

Thinking happens in the mental world or the mind. The thoughts that can be produced in the mind are unlimited and eternal.

Any thought as insignificant as it might seem is bound to produce an effect sooner or later.

Now as a human being who do you think you are? A doctor, a musician, a football player?

The biggest problem in Africa, in the community we live in is that when we don't see the possibility of us attaining what we want,we get discouraged. We try to find any job just to survive or turn to crime. We live under the illusion that making money is the solution to our problem.

The real problem is if we don't grow spiritually first, and the material grows as a result, we will never be satisfied. Bearing in mind that growing spiritually implies thinking properly, positively.

We are all so accustomed to thinking negatively and it is really no one's fault. Most of the programs on TV, the newspapers talk about crime, rape and how the rich got richer. In our daily conversation all those things tend to come up very often. Even if we tried to think positively, we so often find ourselves overwhelmed with all that negativity. All those negative thoughts also manifest as negative events and bad circumstances. They make poverty, decease , suffering look real.

How does thought wrap itself up in matter, how does it take form?

In nature every single element seeks to express itself. From dead matter to living entities this truth remains unchanged.

Every single element follows certain patterns or natural laws in order for them to find a way to express.

That expression is obviously the reason why that particular element comes to life.

As insignificant as it may seem, all that exist has got a good reason why it came into existence.

Finding a way to way to express allows other living entities to become what they are meant to be.

Science teaches us that the smallest element in nature is called an atom. The atom is made of a nucleus and electrons floating around it. Any solid object that you and I see right now, can actually be broken down to the size of an atom. In reverse everything is made up of a bunch of atoms that form molecules and molecules form tissues and finally tissues into material bodies.

Everything that we see, touch or experience in one way or another is made up of the same basic element: the atom.

There is an intelligence that is directing all the atoms in the universe to combine and form the shapes that we see in our everyday life.

Somehow every atom knows where to go with no apparent force guiding it. It is attracted to certain body at a certain time to fulfill a role. It knows what to do.

Let take a little journey into our imagination and look at any beautiful flower. It naturally starts off as a seed in the ground. Conditions have to be met in order for the seed to spring into life. There must be enough water, the soil must be fertile, the temperature must be moderate for the plant to start growing. The seed will absorb water and start growing roots which will sink in the soil to look for nutrients. The plant has to grow leaves so it can absorb energy from the sun. The plant will find itself at it prime when the beautiful flowers appear. Taking a good look at those flowers clearly demonstrates that every atom in that flower traveled long journeys to come and help the plant show off its beauty. After fulfilling that role, they will go on to play another role somewhere else. When the flower dies after a few days the atoms' job is done. their purpose in that moment was to express beauty.

In the process of expressing beauty in the case of the flower, so many elements are brought into play. The thought is a beautiful flower, the element that that come into play are: the wind, the rain, the sun, the soil.... Just to name a few.

When a thought of growth is held in the mind, it energizes atoms and so many other elements in the whole universe. It gives them purpose. The whole universe is mind at rest. Once there is a disturbance it seeks to regain its balance. The necessary elements will be mobilized and given the purpose of clothing the thought in matter. Help the thought to express itself, and go back to rest. Is there any proof to this theory? All I can say is it can be experienced.

Finding one's purpose is the easiest thing to do. A simple question should help it: what do you like? Eating? Sleeping? Reading? cleaning? For every like there is a job in store for it. What one was born with as talent is the purpose they should be fulfilling. We have gotten so accustomed to just finding a job, make money, spent it and go look for more money. Not only have we lost our roots, we are also lost to ourselves. Wandering in the wilderness of modern life trying to find our bearings, trying to survive. It is not normal we should be living.

African culture is based on unity: “one finger can’t do much but 10 can lift a heavy rock” oneness with the whole of humanity and nature is our true strength.

Finding a purpose, be it insignificant or big, makes us what we are. Make us fit within the grandiose scheme we call universe and makes us reconnect to our real origin, GOD.

True African culture has nothing to do the buildings we living in or the clothes we wear. It is that inner connection to our ancestors that is expressed through music, dance and unity.

Thinking right is the one thing school doesn't teach. Religion should but these days it is also defective. It takes a great effort to think correctly. You have to make a great effort to notice what happening inside your head. It takes concentration. But if it is done daily it becomes easy.

There are millions of thoughts that float in our heads daily. It is impossible to notice all of them. Remembering to observe how they float from time to time at first is enough.

One day you could be able to notice what you were thinking when someone insulted you. Then maybe notice what you were thinking about when you forgot your wallet at home. Then it gets easier and easier.

Tracing the origin of the thoughts will come naturally. The more you notice the thoughts, the more curious you become to find out where they actually originate. The phase “what was I thinking?” won’t just come to your mouth to express frustration. It will come as a shock when for example you thought of hurting a person because your partner looked at them with greedy eyes. It should be your partner’s fault, not his. The cause in this case is unfounded jealousy.

Jealousy is one of the egos. One of the my-selves that can change your personality into a violent person. it is a false self that must disappear. True and sincere fast should do the trick. Intense prayer can help when it is really sincere.

The domain of the inner self in not ours. The force that govern it is beyond our grasp. We can only pray and make an effort to change. The inner self is in a deep abyss surrounded by many egos. The more we pray for the elimination of defective selves the more space they will give us to perceive our true self. It doesn't happen in one day.

As energy wasted towards an ego no longer flaws the wrong way, it will be diverted towards recreating a new self and repair the rusted connection between man and the inner being who is the same as God in quality. Then the individual will actually know God.

The balance between the horizontal and the vertical lines creates a beautiful rose at the centre. The bed that will carry the child Christ. May anyone who read this book find himself within truly.

Slavery and colonization have not have not ended. Those two concepts have just evolved. We are now slaves of money and power. As an African person money and power are presented in front of us as bait. As something that we have to obtain and yet it is impossible to reach by normal means. We have a continent full of dreamers, hungry ghosts.

Being free means breaking the chains that bind us to a false sense of self. It means to reconnect to our inner being and find our purpose.

www.ingramcontent.com/pod-product-compliance
Lightning Source LLC
LaVergne TN
LVHW012113160826
845678LV00014B/3063

9798844015960